Dealing with
Disorders and Disease

Multiple Sclerosis

Published in 2025 by **Cheriton Children's Books**
1 Bank Drive West, Shrewsbury, Shropshire, SY3 9DJ

First Edition

Author: Sarah Eason
Designer: Paul Myerscough
Editor: Jennifer Sanderson
Proofreader: Ellie James

Picture credits: Cover illustration by Doodle Press. Inside: p4: Shutterstock/Jacob Lund, p6: Shutterstock/Jaojormami, p7: Shutterstock/SeventyFour, p9b: Shutterstock/Designua, p9t: Shutterstock/Minerva Studio, p10: Shutterstock/Javi Indy, p11: Shutterstock/Reshetnikov_art, p12: Shutterstock/Nikkimeel, p13: Shutterstock/SeventyFour, p14: Shutterstock/Monkey Business Images, p16: Shutterstock/Kateryna Kon, p19b: Shutterstock/MMD Creative, p19t: Shutterstock/Oliveromg, p20: Shutterstock/Martin Novak, p21: Shutterstock/Andy Dean Photography, p22b: Shutterstock/Teerayuth Oanwong, p22t: Shutterstock/Vitstudio, p24: Shutterstock/CI Photos, p25: Shutterstock/Terelyuk, p26: Shutterstock/Monkey Business Images, p29b: Shutterstock/Antonio Guillem, p29t: Shutterstock/Jose Luis Calvo, p30: Shutterstock/Ground Picture, p31: Shutterstock/Fizkes, p33: Shutterstock/Pheelings Media, p35: Shutterstock/Yurii_Yarema, p36: Shutterstock/VesnaArt, p37: Shutterstock/Daisy Daisy, p38: Shutterstock/Peter Porrini, p39: Shutterstock/SvetaZi, p41: Shutterstock/Kamil Macniak, p42b: Shutterstock/Atstock Productions, p42t: Shutterstock/Goodluz, p43: Shutterstock/Reshetnikov Art, p44: Shutterstock/Mariia Korneeva, p45b: Shutterstock/New Africa, p45t: Shutterstock/Fizkes, p46: Shutterstock/Fizkes, p47: Shutterstock/Fizkes, p48: Shutterstock/Carballo, p51: Shutterstock/Todja, p53b: Shutterstock/Pong Handsome, p53t: Shutterstock/AS Photo Family, p55b: Shutterstock/Andrey Popov, p55t: Shutterstock/Pikselstock, p56: Shutterstock/Pressmaster, p58: Shutterstock/Fizkes.

Disclaimer: The photographs shown in this book are intended to support the factual content. The publisher notes that the individuals shown in the photographs do not necessarily have the condition/s described in the book.

Printed in China

Contents

CHAPTER 1
Multiple Sclerosis 4
Education and Multiple Sclerosis 12
Dealing with Education 14

CHAPTER 2
Why Multiple Sclerosis Happens 16
Social Connections and Multiple Sclerosis 30
Dealing with Social Connections 32

CHAPTER 3
Getting a Diagnosis 34

CHAPTER 4
Help with Multiple Sclerosis 40
Mental Health and Multiple Sclerosis 46
Dealing with Mental Health 48

CHAPTER 5
Living with Multiple Sclerosis 50
Employment and Multiple Sclerosis 54
Dealing with Employment 56

CONCLUSION
Multiple Sclerosis and the Future 58

Glossary 60
Find Out More 63
Index and About the Author 64

CHAPTER 1

Multiple Sclerosis

Have you ever felt exhausted after a long hike, or so numb in the legs after sitting cross-legged for a while that you cannot walk, or dizzy after getting off an amusement park ride? Have you ever felt a sudden desperate need to use the toilet, or stumbled over your speech? Some people may feel or experience all of these things together most of the time, along with pain, intolerance to heat, and many other symptoms, or signs of illness. They feel this way because they have multiple sclerosis, also known as MS.

Understanding the Nervous System

People with multiple sclerosis experience so many varied symptoms around the body because it is a disease that affects their nervous system. The nervous system is a network of nerves through our bodies that carry information to and from the body's control center—the brain. Information comes from outside the body via the senses of touch, taste, hearing, vision, and smell. Information also comes from internal organs such as the stomach, perhaps that it is empty and food is required, or the bladder, because it is full and needs emptying.

An Information Superhighway

The spinal cord is around 18 inches (46 cm) long and up to half an inch (1.3 cm) thick, and it is the superhighway of the nerve world. It funnels information speedily and directly toward and away from the brain so it can communicate with the rest of the body. Millions of neurons in the brain send signals throughout the body to control movement, sensation, memory, understanding, and speech. Peripheral nerves around the body connect up with the spinal cord, tucked safely away in the spine. These nerves carry sensation, such as pain, around the body.

What Is Multiple Sclerosis?

Multiple sclerosis happens when neurons in the central nervous system (CNS) become damaged so they cannot carry out their normal work. Because multiple sclerosis affects nerves, we say that it is a neurological disease. Globally, around 2.9 million people have multiple sclerosis. People do not catch the disease or inherit it directly through their genes. Many factors, including infections, their genes, and even where they are from, all help determine whether they get the disease. Multiple sclerosis is a progressive disease because it usually worsens over time. Its course is unpredictable because symptoms vary widely from person to person. Symptoms can improve or periodically become worse through a person's life.

You probably know someone with multiple sclerosis because it is relatively common. Nearly 3 million people around the world have the condition. In the United States, around 1 million adults live with multiple sclerosis. This has doubled since 1975. In this book, we will look at what causes multiple sclerosis, how it can be treated, and what it is like to live with this condition.

"The symptoms of multiple sclerosis may come and go or worsen over time, depending on the individual and the course of their disease."

Every time people take a step, blink, or move their arms, their brain and spinal cord are at work, together forming the CNS.

Symptoms of Multiple Sclerosis

Multiple sclerosis is highly variable. Two people with the disease may have very different signs and symptoms. Their range of symptoms can also change over time, depending where the nerves are being affected. However, some symptoms are more common than others and are experienced by many people with multiple sclerosis. Symptoms include:

Fatigue and weakness: These symptoms affect energy levels, which can have an impact on a person's ability to work and study.

Spasticity: This means feeling stiff and having uncontrolled muscle twitches or spasms, most commonly in the legs.

Numbness or tingling: Multiple sclerosis may cause a person to feel numbness in the face, body, or limbs.

Dizziness: This is when someone feels unbalanced or light-headed, as though they are about to collapse.

Walking difficulties: This symptom results from weakness in leg and feet muscles, dizziness affecting balance, numbness in the feet, and spasticity.

Pain: More than half of all people with multiple sclerosis feel the sensation of pain in their bodies, even when there is no direct stimulus to cause it.

Bladder and bowel problems: People with multiple sclerosis often experience incontinence and constipation.

Emotional and cognitive changes: People may experience strong mood swings, depression and other emotional changes, and/or a changing ability to process and learn information or focus attention.

Along with the common symptoms described on this page, people may also experience less-frequent symptoms such as slurred speech, problems swallowing or breathing, headaches, itching, and seizures.

Some people are so severely affected by multiple sclerosis that they need to use a wheelchair to help them move around.

Understanding Multiple Sclerosis

Most people with multiple sclerosis experience symptoms over days or weeks, followed by periods of remission during which symptoms get better. Then they may have further relapses of previous symptoms or experience new symptoms. This pattern is called relapsing-remitting multiple sclerosis. Around two-thirds of the people with relapsing-remitting multiple sclerosis experience shorter remission periods and symptoms that gradually become worse. This pattern is called secondary-progressive multiple sclerosis. Around 10 to 15 percent of multiple sclerosis sufferers experience continuous symptoms with no remissions. This pattern of the disease is called primary-progressive multiple sclerosis.

Damage to Myelin

The name multiple sclerosis means "many scars." It was given that name because doctors examining patients with the disease spotted visibly hardened scar areas, or plaques, dotted through their CNS. Plaques are caused by damage to neurons or, more specifically, to a substance called myelin that coats them.

What Is Myelin?

If you have ever seen telephone cables, you may have noticed that they are thin and covered with plastic sleeves. An electric current runs through the cable's inner metal core. The plastic is an insulating material that stops the signal from escaping through the sides. If it escaped, it could lose information or slow down its transmission speed. Myelin around the axon, the fiber part of a neuron, has the same job.

What Does Myelin Do?

Myelin allows a nerve to pass electrical impulses rapidly to the next neuron without losing the signal. In the CNS, efficient impulses allow effortless, speedy, and coordinated movements through the body. When myelin is lost from CNS neurons, however, impulses get disrupted. In turn, information to and from the brain and to muscles and other tissues can become garbled. This botched transmission causes the many symptoms of multiple sclerosis.

Caused by the Immune System

Multiple sclerosis is said to be an immune-mediated disease because it is caused by the immune system. In a properly functioning immune system, white blood cells move to infection locations and gobble up invading bacteria and viruses so they do not cause further damage to the body. Sometimes, however, people have diseases in which the immune system changes its behavior and starts to attack normal healthy cells in the body rather than invaders. Multiple sclerosis is one such disease.

Attacking the Nervous System

In multiple sclerosis, T-cells and other white blood cells start to attack and destroy myelin on CNS neurons. They also attack cells near neurons called oligodendrocytes, which are myelin factories for axons. Plaques in the CNS result from such immune attacks. Their location affects the symptoms they cause. For example, plaques in the part of the spinal cord nearest the legs may affect walking, but those in the speech center of the brain may have an effect on a person's ability to speak clearly.

If nerves that affect walking are attacked by the immune system, it can mean that people lose their mobility.

Understanding Multiple Sclerosis

In relapsing-remitting multiple sclerosis, oligodendrocytes can recover between waves of immune attack and recoat neurons with myelin. Then plaques can heal and symptoms can go away. But repeated attacks in the same places can eventually wipe out oligodendrocytes and even damage axons stripped of myelin. In progressive forms of the disease, permanent plaques may remain that affect brain activity and can even stop whole nerves from working, permanently affecting movements and body functions.

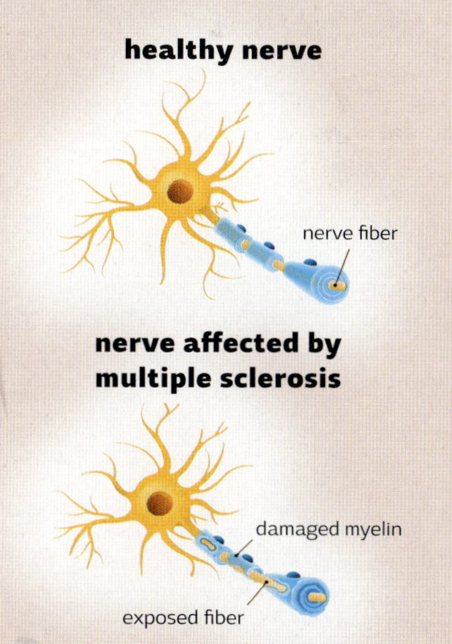

In general, people of northern European origin are at a slightly higher risk of developing multiple sclerosis than people of Asian, Native American, or African descent.

Looking for Patterns

Anyone can develop multiple sclerosis when their immune system goes out of control. Although the disease can strike at any age, it most commonly occurs between 20 and 50 years of age. However, scientists called epidemiologists looked at the backgrounds and medical histories of people with multiple sclerosis. They noticed patterns in the spread of the disease among the global population. Where you are from, your ethnic group, and your gender appear to make a difference in whether you will develop multiple sclerosis.

The Impact of Climate

Multiple sclerosis is generally more common in people who live farther from the equator. This is the imaginary central horizontal line around our planet where temperatures are highest, on average. Points on the equator receive more intense sunlight as the sun can be directly overhead. The frequency of the disease increases heading north or south from the equator, into areas with cooler temperatures, less sunlight, and shorter summers.

The Role of Ethnicity

An ethnic group is often defined as people with shared ancestral, social, and even physical characteristics, often from particular areas on Earth. Some ethnic groups have a lower- or higher-than-normal risk of developing multiple sclerosis. For example, many Sami and Inuit people traditionally live inside the Arctic circle, far from the equator, yet have low risk of developing the disease. Multiple sclerosis is virtually unheard of in Australian Aborigines. Some people, such as Parsis of India and Palestinians, live near the equator, yet have a higher-than-normal risk of developing multiple sclerosis.

Facing Facts

Females are at far greater risk of developing multiple sclerosis than males. Some scientists believe that hormonal differences may be a reason for this, especially since the disease usually shows up after puberty, when there are great hormonal changes in girls.

If you are female, then you have around four times the risk that a male has of developing multiple sclerosis.

Understanding Multiple Sclerosis

A 2014 study found a clue to why more women than men develop multiple sclerosis. Researchers found that females susceptible to, or at risk of, multiple sclerosis produce higher levels of a protein called S1PR2 than males do. They also found that the highest levels of that protein are found in areas of the brain that are usually damaged by multiple sclerosis. The protein helps control whether immune cells move from blood vessels into the brain. With more protein, more cells invade the brain and cause more inflammation and myelin damage.

Education and Multiple Sclerosis

Although multiple sclerosis is unusual in children, it can sometimes occur in childhood and the teenage years. That then has an impact on life at school for teens and children affected by the disease. For young people at college with the condition, the experience can also be very challenging and make ongoing education difficult.

MAKING LEARNING DIFFICULT

Cognitive problems related to multiple sclerosis, such as difficulties with memory, focus, and processing information can affect a person's academic performance. People with the disease can find studying, remembering information, completing assignments, and performing well in exams hard due to the effects of the disease.

Fatigue because of multiple sclerosis can interfere with school or college attendance. It also affects joining in with class activities and discussions when present.

Problems with Brain Function

Cognitive problems related to multiple sclerosis can affect a person's academic performance. They include:

Problems with memory:
Multiple sclerosis can cause difficulties with both short-term and long-term memory. People may experience problems remembering information given in class or recalling details needed for exams and assignments.

Problems with concentration: The disease can affect attention span and concentration, making it difficult for people to focus during lectures, study sessions, or while completing academic tasks.

Problems with processing information: Multiple sclerosis can slow down the speed at which people can process information, which means it takes longer to take on board information given in classes or while studying for assignments.

Problems with planning: It can be difficult for people to plan, organize, problem-solve, and make decisions because of the drastic effect of the disease on their brain.

PROBLEMS WITH GETTING AROUND

Mobility problems caused by weakness, spasticity in muscles, and balance issues can make it very difficult to move about school and college campuses and join in with extracurricular activities. Campuses also may not be fully accessible for people with mobility issues, for example, they may not have modifications for wheelchair users. Accessibility barriers, such as stairs, uneven ground, or lack of elevators all make getting around difficult.

TALKING ABOUT IT

Sometimes, it can be very difficult for young people with multiple sclerosis to know how to discuss their condition with teachers and other staff in educational settings. People with the disease may be concerned about how they will be perceived if they talk about their illness, perhaps worrying that they will not be seen in a positive light.

Young people with multiple sclerosis may not want to talk to other students about the disease due to worries about stigma or misconceptions about it.

Dealing with Education

There are many ways in which young people with multiple sclerosis can be helped at school or college. By putting support in place and creating an inclusive environment, barriers to learning can be minimized. Awareness of the disease and the limitations it puts on students is very important, so that going to school or college is made more accessible. With the right structure and support in place, young people with the disease can achieve.

KEEPING LEARNING FLEXIBLE

Flexibility with learning really helps young people with multiple sclerosis. That can include extended time for exams and being able to choose where to sit in a classroom or a lecture hall. Flexibility around attendance can mean students have more time at home and a lighter timetable. Today, teachers and support staff at schools and colleges work closely with students with multiple sclerosis to create personalized learning plans based on their needs. That helps students put in place a structure that works for them so they can manage their education in the best way.

It is important that learning plans are flexible and monitored so that changes can be put in place as needed.

THE POWER OF TECHNOLOGY

Using assistive technology tools can help students with multiple sclerosis overcome mental and physical barriers in school and college. Tools such as speech-to-text software and adaptive keyboards make it easier to deal with physical limitations that can get in the way of learning.

UNDERSTANDING THE DISEASE

Students with multiple sclerosis manage their education in the same way that they manage the other areas of their life—by monitoring their symptoms and making adjustments where needed. Taking breaks to rest and recharge is important so that fatigue is controlled and people do not become overwhelmed by the academic day. In times that are especially stressful—for example, during exams—it can help to use stress-management techniques such as mindfulness or relaxation exercises.

Offering flexibility with class schedules and assignment deadlines helps students manage changes in symptoms and energy levels.

Strategies such as help with taking notes, extra time for exams, or alternative ways of assessing work can help young people with multiple sclerosis overcome any difficulties.

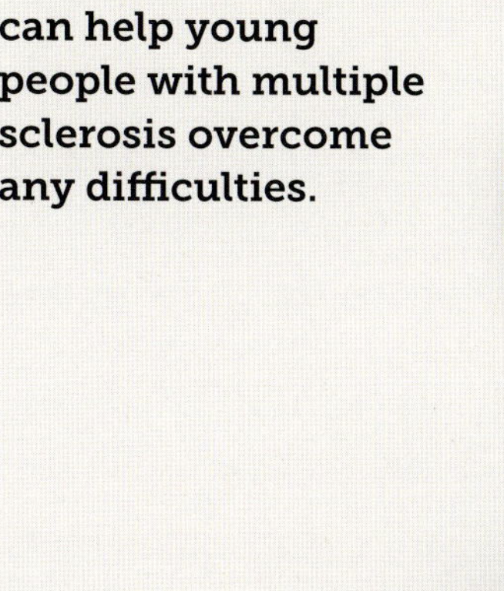

CHAPTER 2

Why Multiple Sclerosis Happens

When someone gets bitten by a mosquito carrying the malaria parasite, they will usually develop a disease called malaria, which brings on dangerous fevers. When someone breathes in Mycobacterium tuberculosis bacteria, they will often develop the lung disease tuberculosis (TB). In both cases, the disease has a clear cause. However, multiple sclerosis is different because several factors may be involved in causing the disease, and the factors may interact in complicated ways. Scientists are researching the causes of multiple sclerosis in the hope of finding better ways to treat the disease.

Can Infections Cause Disease?

Scientists suspect that some infections can cause multiple sclerosis. From birth, when bacteria or viruses enter our bodies, they attack cells. Our bodies normally trigger an immune response to the attacks. White blood cells eat the invaders and also produce antibodies. Antibodies are proteins that have a chemical that is made to fight a chemical on those specific invaders. Antibodies can damage or destroy invaders. They can also help our bodies recognize the threats so they can be dealt with more easily during any future attacks. Scientists have found that antibodies to some viruses and bacteria are found in larger amounts in people with multiple sclerosis than in people without the disease.

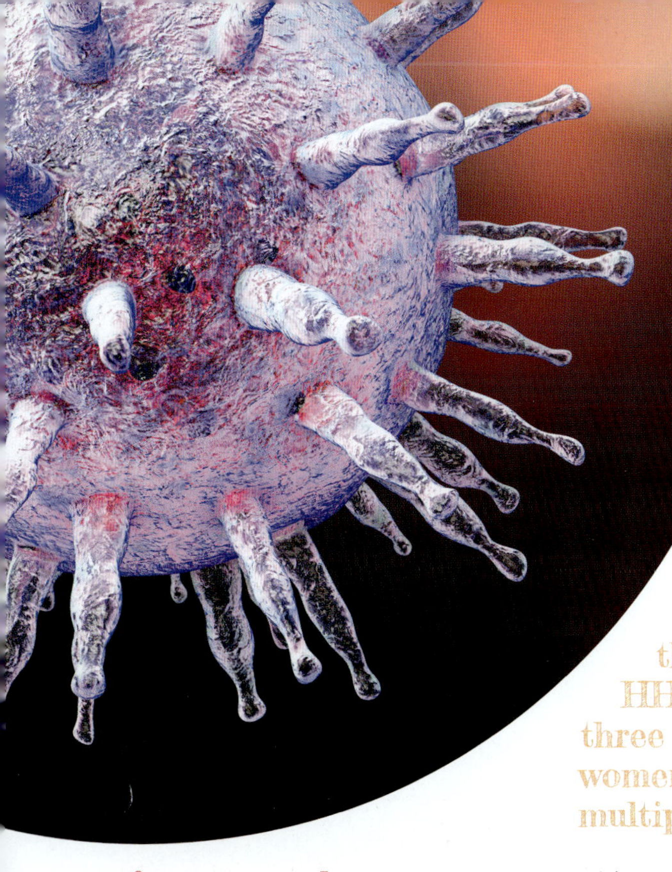

EBV is often associated with people suffering from multiple sclerosis. Because the tiny virus hides in the human body, the risk of flare-ups persists for years after catching the virus.

"One study found that levels of the HHV-6A antibody were three times higher in women with progressive multiple sclerosis."

Viruses and Bacteria Linked to Multiple Sclerosis

Several possible viruses and bacteria may contribute to the development of multiple sclerosis, including the measles virus and pneumonia bacteria. But the most likely are:

Mono virus: Mononucleosis, or mono, is often called the "kissing" disease due to the way it often spreads among younger people. It is actually caused by the Epstein-Barr virus, or EBV. EBV infection is characterized by fatigue, rash, fever, sore throat, swollen neck glands, and other symptoms. Antibodies to EBV are a lot higher in people with multiple sclerosis, indicating that they have been exposed to the disease. It therefore appears that being infected with mono increases the risk of having multiple sclerosis.

Human herpes virus 6 (HHV-6): The term HHV-6 actually refers to two closely related viruses: HHV-6A and HHV-6B. The B form infects nearly everyone on Earth, usually before the age of three, and usually causes mild fever, diarrhea, and a rash called roseola. The A form is rarer. Both types stay in people, doing nothing for long periods of time after initial infection. They sometimes cause health problems later on. HHV-6A is a trigger for relapses of multiple sclerosis.

Environmental Causes

The environment we live in can have a big effect on our lives and health. For example, living in a home in which someone smokes can increase the chances of having lung and heart problems. Epidemiologists have concluded that various environmental factors, from smoke exposure to sunlight levels, can contribute to the development of multiple sclerosis.

Vitamin D Is Key

One vital vitamin is vitamin D. It helps our bodies absorb food nutrients such as calcium, and supports our immune responses. Most of our vitamin D is produced naturally in the skin when exposed to sunlight. People who live closer to the equator get greater amounts of sunlight all year. They have higher levels of the vitamin than people farther from the equator.

Understanding Multiple Sclerosis

Children and teenagers with low vitamin D have an increased risk of developing multiple sclerosis in later life. This effect has also been found in newborns, suggesting that vitamin D levels in a mother during pregnancy might affect a child's future risk of multiple sclerosis. Children born in the northern hemisphere in May are in early development inside their mothers during the darkest, lowest vitamin D times of year. Mothers of children born in November are exposed to more sunlight at a critical time of their pregnancy, so children born in May have a greater risk than children born in November.

Facing Facts

Families and individuals migrate for many reasons, such as escaping danger or abuse, or seeking better work. Several studies have shown that when people younger than 15 years of age migrate from a sunny region to a less-sunny region, they gain a higher risk of developing multiple sclerosis. The opposite is true of teenagers born in a high-risk area moving to a low-risk, sunnier place. If migration happens after age 15, a person's risk of developing multiple sclerosis does not change.

Children who travel to a sunny place to live before they reach their mid-teens are less likely to develop multiple sclerosis, even though they were born in the northern hemisphere where risk of getting the disease is greater.

Environmental Research

Researchers have explored many possible causes of multiple sclerosis, including environmental factors. That is because some people with the disease found that they first had symptoms after being exposed to something new in their environment. Scientists have researched the following environmental factors to find out if they may trigger multiple sclerosis:

- Environmental allergies
- Exposure to household pets
- Exposure to heavy metals, including lead, manganese, and mercury
- Chemical solvents such as paints

The research showed no link between the above environmental factors and multiple sclerosis.

There is also no evidence that having allergies, owning a dog, eating artificial sweeteners, or suffering physical trauma, can make people develop multiple sclerosis!

Genetic Causes

Some diseases, such as cystic fibrosis, are inherited. This means that people can only develop cystic fibrosis if their parents pass on the genes that cause it. This is not true of multiple sclerosis. However, people can still inherit genes that make it more likely they might develop the disease.

What Are Genes?

Genes store coded instructions that tell cells to make proteins, which affect everything from the color of your hair to how you grow and your health. Every cell in our bodies contains a complete set of these instructions as sequences of chemicals, which are stored in the chromosomes in cells. Each gene in a chromosome has specialized sequence patterns, providing the code to do particular jobs.

Male and Female

Male sex cells (sperm) and female sex cells (ova, or eggs) each contain just one copy of each chromosome, or 23 chromosomes in total. During sexual reproduction, a sperm fertilizes or joins with an egg and the chromosomes of both pair up to make 46 in the developing baby. During this process, slight variations in sequences can occur that cause the baby to have subtly different genes from its parents. Usually, such mutations are not a problem, but sometimes genetic changes can have an impact on health.

Gene Mutations in Common

In 2016, Canadian scientists examining seven patients with multiple sclerosis from two unrelated families found that both carried the same gene mutation. Normal copies of the NR1H3 gene produce a protein called LXRA, which helps control inflammation of cells and tissues, and helps in the production of myelin. Having the variant makes multiple sclerosis more likely. Other scientists are unsure whether the NR1H3 variant is a major cause since it is also found in people without the disease. However, the Canadian scientists believe this variant may make someone more likely to develop the disease than someone who has the normal version.

Scientists are constantly learning more about genes and hereditary disease. While genes may put people at a greater risk of developing diseases, their environment also plays a large factor.

Understanding Multiple Sclerosis

People who have a parent with multiple sclerosis have a 2 percent higher risk of developing the disease than someone in the general population. The risk rises to 4 percent if they have a sibling, or brother or sister, with the disease and 30 percent if they have an identical twin with the disease. This is because of the genes they have inherited in common. These people might live completely normal lives. But they might also experience changes to their immune systems because of environmental factors that trigger the mutations. If this occurs, they progress to developing multiple sclerosis.

What Is Gene Therapy?

Scientists studying cells from thousands of patients with multiple sclerosis have identified more than around 200 genes that are involved in the disease. The hope in the future is that scientists will be able to replace mutations with normal copies of genes to help prevent or cure the condition. This type of treatment is called gene therapy.

Replacing Mutated Genes

The most common gene therapy method uses modified viruses to transport replacement sections of DNA into chromosomes in cells. Scientists in a laboratory remove any of the virus's own genes that could cause sicknesses in people. They then replace them with the normal functioning gene to be added in the gene therapy procedure. The viruses then enter cells and "infect" them with the normal gene, replacing the mutated gene. The corrected cells are injected into the patient to replace faulty cells and spread copies of the normal gene.

Replacement sections of DNA could provide a cure for diseases such as multiple sclerosis.

Gene Therapy and Multiple Sclerosis

In diseases such as cystic fibrosis, a single, identified gene mutation is responsible. The idea of using gene therapy in such situations is reasonable. However, multiple sclerosis is much more complicated, partly because it involves many genes as possible mutation sites. But those genes interact in complex ways, and are only activated after particular environmental triggers, such as vitamin D levels.

Understanding Multiple Sclerosis

A problem common to most gene therapy is that introduced cells containing viruses can be recognized as intruders and be attacked by a patient's immune system. In the CNS, introduced neurons might trigger increased T-cell attack, with greater loss of myelin and worsening of the symptoms of multiple sclerosis. Despite these obstacles, scientists are carefully studying the activities of different genes in search of key genes that might be suitable for gene therapy in the future.

Testing a Theory

Scientists at the University of Florida tested a possible gene therapy for multiple sclerosis on mice. They injected into their liver modified viruses carrying the normal copy of a gene responsible for myelin production in the brain. The liver is part of the body's immune system, acting as a kind of school to educate T-cells that regulate immune attacks by other T-cells. They hoped that if the liver can recognize the virus as harmless, it will spark production of T-cells that suppress attacks on cells making myelin in the CNS. This approach was successful and some neurological symptoms were reversed in the mice.

What Is Stem Cell Therapy?

Researchers are exploring whether it is possible to introduce new cells into people with multiple sclerosis to slow their disease activity, repair existing damage, or replace faulty parts of the nervous or immune systems. This therapy is not yet available for multiple sclerosis. But it is already in use to treat conditions such as leukemia, or cancer of the blood.

Creating Special Cells

Muscles contain muscle cells, some of which can change shape to allow muscle contraction and relaxation. Intestines are lined with cells that absorb nutrients from digested food into the blood. Red blood cells carry oxygen to other cells for respiration. These cells and most other cells in the body are specialized with very specific functions. Some cells, however, are unspecialized. Called stem cells, they have the potential to develop into one of a number of different specialized cell types, depending on the body's needs at a particular time.

Making Copies

One of the great things about stem cells is that they can make copies of themselves. Most specialized cells cannot do this, but one stem cell can split over and over to produce millions of cells over many months. This can be made to happen in glass dishes in laboratories, not just inside a human body. Scientists speed up the process by adding chemicals in a growth solution so stem cells divide more quickly. Then they can make a lot of copies of the stem cells that they need for use in therapies.

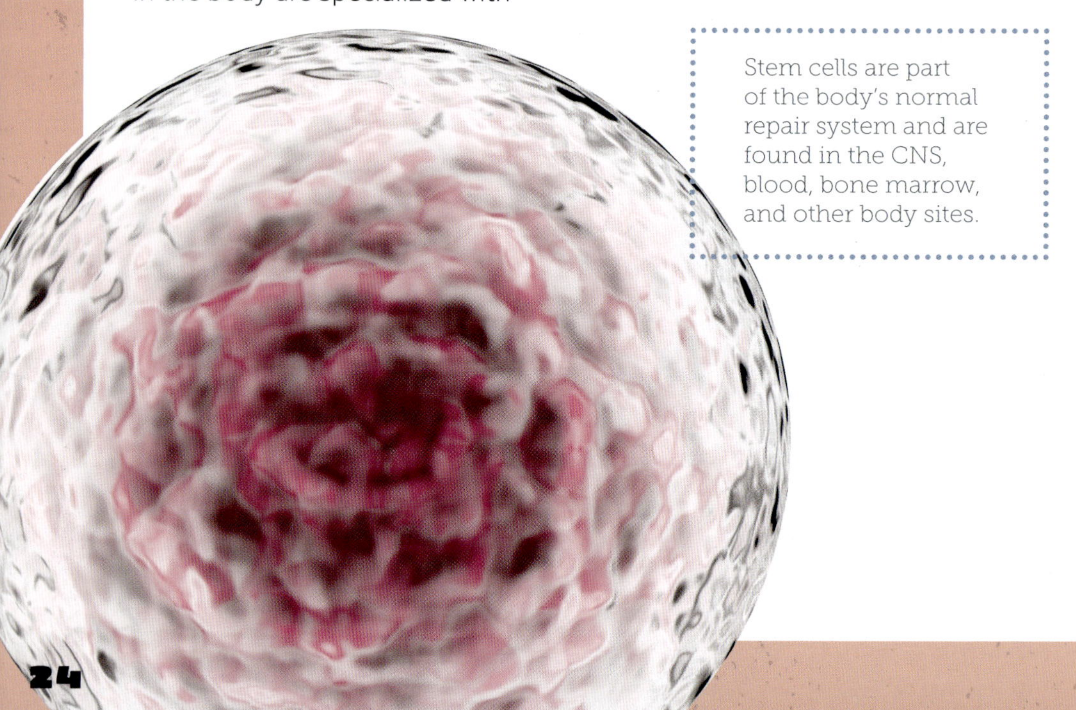

Stem cells are part of the body's normal repair system and are found in the CNS, blood, bone marrow, and other body sites.

Understanding Multiple Sclerosis

In the future, doctors and neurologists may be able to offer stem cell therapy to replace faulty, damaged, or missing cells in the immune system or in the CNS. There are several experimental strategies. One uses cells in bone marrow, or in the fat layer beneath the skin, to protect CNS cells from disease processes and to promote repair. However, the strategy that has been studied the most and that is currently in trial, is very drastic. It involves completely rebooting the immune system so it no longer attacks the brain and spinal cord to cause further damage. This is called autologous hematopoietic stem cell transplantation, or AHSCT. AHSCT uses powerful drugs to wipe out harmful cells in the immune system of a patient with multiple sclerosis. It then rebuilds a new immune system using stem cells previously collected from the patient's blood.

Stem cell therapy is already used for certain diseases, but it could become a radical way to treat multiple sclerosis too.

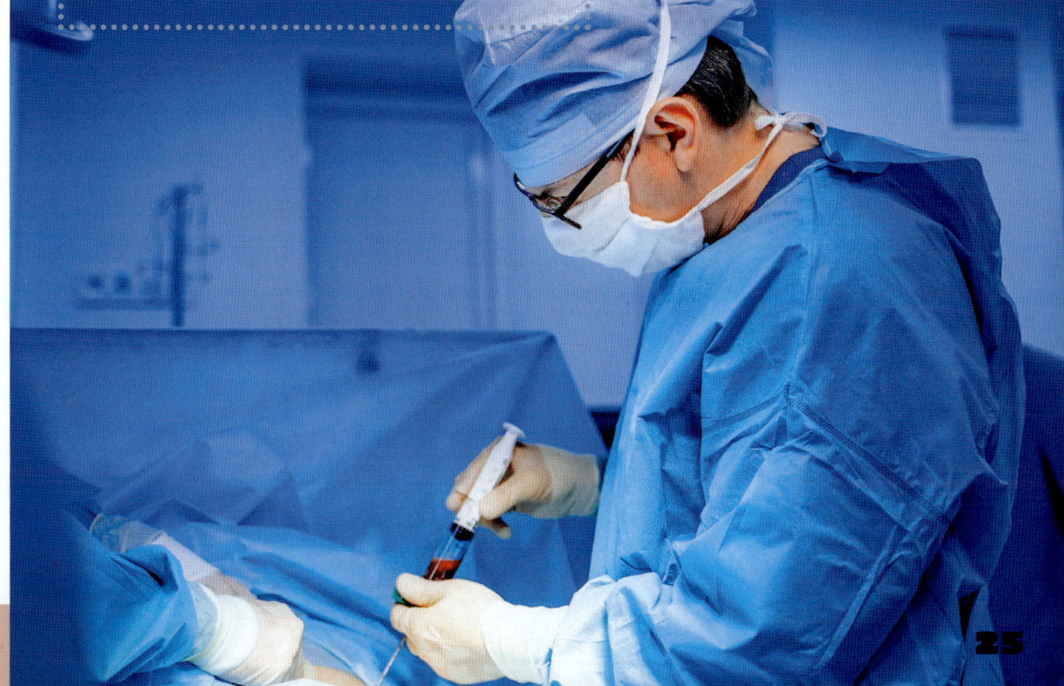

A Risky Procedure

The AHSCT procedure is complex and involves several steps. It is risky for patients. Doctors recommend it mostly for people with relapsing multiple sclerosis in which there is active inflammation of the CNS, rather than for those with significant disability and progressive forms of the disease.

Step 1—Mobilization: The blood only contains a small number of stem cells naturally, but many are needed for AHSCT. The first step is to encourage stem cells to increase in number and move from the bone marrow into the blood. This is done using drugs delivered into a patient's veins through a drip and injections.

Step 2—Harvesting: After about 10 days, the patient has a blood test to confirm there are enough stem cells. Then a needle is put in the patient's arm and attached to a cell separator machine. Blood circulates through the machine as it separates out the stem cells and returns the rest of the blood to the patient's body. The harvested stem cells are then frozen until they are to be transplanted back into the patient in the hospital.

Step 3—Chemotherapy: The use of strong drugs to kill cells is called chemotherapy. In AHSCT, chemotherapy is used to destroy the T-cells and other immune system cells involved in multiple sclerosis. Patients must stay in the hospital for several days while they receive chemotherapy.

Step 4—Transplantation: After the chemotherapy is complete, and any traces of the drug have cleared from the patient's blood, the stored stem cells are thawed and returned to the patient's blood through a drip. This takes a couple of hours. After that, it can take up to 30 days for the stem cells to enter the patient's bone marrow and start to make new blood and immune system cells. These cells should not attack the patient's CNS.

Understanding Multiple Sclerosis

After chemotherapy and transplantation, a patient is very susceptible to infection because they have a much-weakened immune system. They have to stay in an isolation room in the hospital. Healthcare workers keep visitors away and give drugs immediately to treat any infections the patient might develop from viruses already in their system. If infections get out of hand, they can rapidly become life threatening. Patients may also need drugs to treat side effects of chemotherapy, such as nausea, vomiting, and bleeding. Even after their new immune system is up and running, patients feel weak and lack energy, and may take from several months to a year to recover.

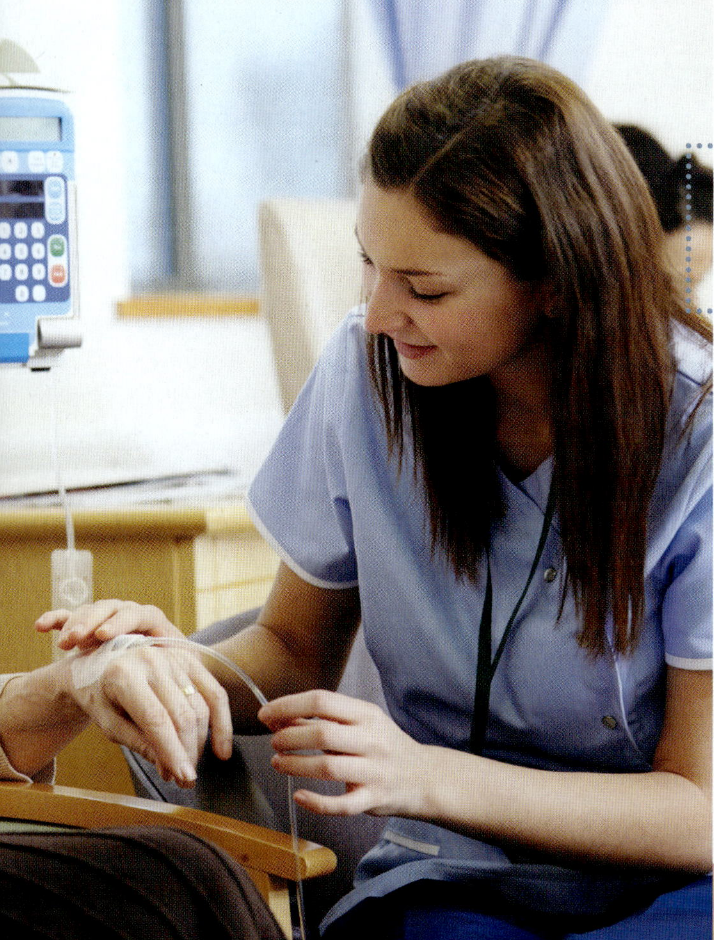

Chemotherapy is often used in cancer treatment to kill cancer cells.

Repairing Damaged Tissue

One possible future stem cell therapy is to repair the damaged CNS tissue of people with multiple sclerosis. Although an exciting idea, it is far from becoming reality. However, other therapies will soon be available to help the CNS repair itself more effectively.

Reprogramming Cells

Stem cell treatment for myelin repair will probably use something called induced pluripotent stem cells, which are specialized cells reprogrammed in laboratories to behave like stem cells. These stem cells could be used to grow enhanced oligodendrocytes that can suppress immune attack and make a lot of myelin. They could then be injected into the CNS to massively increase its potential to make more myelin.

Dealing with Myelin

Oligodendrocytes form from brain stem cells called oligodendrocyte precursor cells (OPCs). Neurons release chemical signals as a "cry for help" when their myelin is damaged. When the signals reach the OPCs, they travel to the site of damage, such as a growing plaque, then transform into mature cells that can produce myelin. Researchers are examining alternative treatments and drugs that can enhance this process in patients with multiple sclerosis so they can naturally repair their own myelin more effectively. Some of the treatments include:

Biotin: This is a vitamin that activates enzymes in the CNS that help the growth of OPCs into oligodendrocytes and boost their myelin production.

Clemastine: This is antihistamine used to relieve itching in people with chickenpox and eczema. The antihistamine enters the brain and causes drowsiness, but it also suppresses the activity of T-cells. In people with multiple sclerosis, this could reduce immune system damage to myelin by boosting myelin repair.

Anti-LINGO-1: This is an antibody that blocks the activity of a protein found in neurons and oligodendrocytes, resulting in myelin repair. In a trial in 2015, Anti-LINGO-1 was injected into the optic nerves of volunteers with optic neuritis. Their test results were improved over volunteers injected with a liquid without the antibody in it. Other medications with the potential for myelin repair are best known for other uses. One such medication, tamoxifen, is usually prescribed to treat breast cancer. Another, miconazole, is commonly used to treat athlete's foot.

Understanding Multiple Sclerosis

Scientists at Cambridge University in the United Kingdom (UK) identified a vitamin D receptor protein on oligodendrocytes. When activated by vitamin D, the receptor works with another protein to boost myelin production. In a laboratory, blocking the receptor reduced myelin production by around 80 percent. In the future, they believe a myelin repair drug targeting this receptor could help people with multiple sclerosis.

This photograph is highly magnified to show nerve fibers surrounded by myelin.

Vitamin D is known to be a protector against multiple sclerosis. Drug trials involving the vitamin D receptor in the body could hold another key to treating the disease.

Social Connections and Multiple Sclerosis

Social connections play an important role in the mental health and wellbeing of people. However, for many people with multiple sclerosis, maintaining a social life can be very difficult, both because of the physical effects of the condition and the mental toll it can take. The extent to which people are affected often depends on how severe their disease is, how rapidly it is progressing, coping mechanisms they have in place, and the support they receive.

SET BACK BY PHYSICAL ISSUES

The physical symptoms of multiple sclerosis, which include fatigue, weakness, mobility issues, pain, and coordination problems, may make it difficult for people to take part in social activities, go to events, or continue with hobbies and interests that they enjoyed before the onset of the disease. Mobility limitations can affect a person's ability to travel. Problems with accessibility in places, such as lack of wheelchair ramps or accessible restrooms, can make it even harder for people with multiple sclerosis to take part in social activities outside their home.

Finding it difficult to easily leave the home and travel to events can make people feel excluded from normal social life.

PROBLEMS WITH THE BRAIN

The effects of the disease on the brain may make having conversations and joining in with group activities difficult. Individuals with multiple sclerosis may also experience problems with speech and finding the right words. They may have trouble remembering names and faces, which can affect social interactions and relationships.

RELATIONSHIP PROBLEMS

Multiple sclerosis can have a huge impact on relationships with family members, friends, coworkers, and partners. Changes in roles and responsibilities within relationships can cause feelings of frustration and guilt in people with the disease, because they feel they are placing a burden on their loved ones. Dynamics within relationships can also be affected as people struggle to cope with caring for a loved one with multiple sclerosis.

Facing Stigma

Sadly, there is still stigma surrounding disability and chronic illness such as multiple sclerosis. That can make it very difficult for people with the disease to form social connections. If they are faced with negative attitudes, stereotypes, and misconceptions about their disease, it can make them reluctant to try and maintain a social life.

People with multiple sclerosis may worry about how others perceive them, which can affect their confidence and willingness to join in with social activities.

Dealing with Social Connections

Most people with multiple sclerosis find that they need to adjust their expectations of themselves when diagnosed with the disease, and that includes their social interactions. People may also find they need to educate those around them about the realities of the disease and how it is impacting them, from their ability to travel through the effect the disease is having on their cognitive abilities. However, with support from others, people with multiple sclerosis can keep socially active.

SETTING BOUNDARIES

People with the disease usually find that they need to keep an eye on their energy levels and symptoms, and if they are struggling, change social plans as needed. Being able to say "no" to social invitations or expectations is important if fatigue and pain are severe. If mobility is an issue, people can still stay connected to family and friends through phone calls, video chats, and social media.

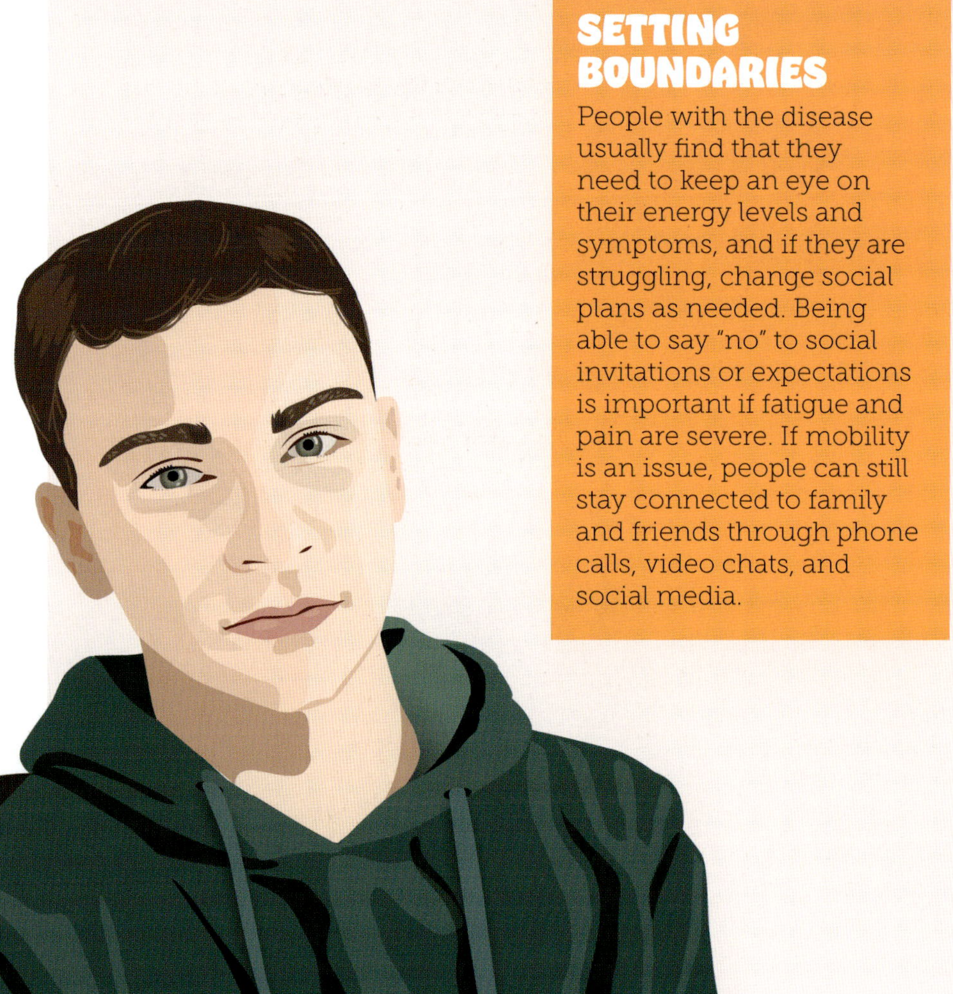

SEEKING SUPPORT

People with multiple sclerosis usually find that seeking out relationships that are supportive and accommodating of their needs is the best way to create a social circle. It is important that they are surrounded by others who respect that there may be times during which a person with multiple sclerosis cannot join in with social events, needs to rest, or is struggling with both their mental and physical health. The best support they can offer is to give physical help when needed and be emotionally supportive when times are tough.

Having open, honest conversations about chronic illnesses such as multiple sclerosis helps educate people so that they can support those affected by the conditions.

Friends, family, and other supporting individuals can help people with multiple sclerosis by respecting their need to change social plans if symptoms make it too difficult to continue with them.

Planning inclusive social gatherings really helps people with multiple sclerosis. For example, meeting in places that are accessible for wheelchair users or are more peaceful if people are feeling tired can make maintaining a social life much easier.

Focusing on quality connections with others, rather than the number of them, can help. It is far better for people with the disease to spend time with a few people who are sympathetic to their needs than try to mix with a wider circle.

Education is the most powerful tool when it comes to helping people with multiple sclerosis. Being aware of the symptoms of multiple sclerosis means people will be more accepting if those with the disease say they cannot meet up.

CHAPTER 3

Getting a Diagnosis

When a patient gets sick, healthcare workers must figure out which disease or condition explains the patient's symptoms and medical history. This is called making a diagnosis. Some conditions are easy to diagnose. However, because multiple sclerosis can cause so many symptoms, diagnosis of this condition is not always simple.

Figuring It Out

Nearly one-third of patients eventually diagnosed with multiple sclerosis first visit their doctor with just one thing they are concerned about. This is often a change in their senses, such as blurred vision, a problem seeing colors, or eye pain typical of optic neuritis. Others may be worried about weakness or loss of sensation in one side of the body, lack of coordination causing them to drop things, or episodes of incontinence. If there are several symptoms typical of multiple sclerosis, a doctor might suspect the disease, even if the symptoms come and go. The doctor will then recommend more tests.

Seeing a Specialist

The next appointment is often with a neurologist, a doctor who is a specialist in nervous system problems. During a neurological examination, the doctor will ask the patient questions about past symptoms to establish a medical history. The neurologist may test for changes in eye movements, senses, limb coordination, balance, reflexes, or speech. Depending on the results, the neurologist may suspect multiple sclerosis even more strongly, and order clinical tests to confirm the diagnosis.

Weakness or loss of sensation in the limbs, hands, and feet can be a sign of multiple sclerosis.

Understanding Multiple Sclerosis

To be able to treat an illness safely and effectively, it is important to know rather than to guess the exact cause of the symptoms. To make a certain diagnosis of multiple sclerosis, doctors must do **all** of these three things:

1 Find evidence of damage to myelin in at least two separate places through the CNS

2 Find evidence that the damage occurred repeatedly over time, at least one month apart

3 Rule out any other causes of the symptoms.

Other Causes of Myelin Damage

Symptoms of multiple sclerosis are caused by loss of myelin. Several other conditions can cause temporary or permanent myelin damage. These include some viral infections, Lyme disease, exposure to heavy metals, vitamin B12 deficiency, and some autoimmune disorders such as AIDS in which the immune system can attack healthy neurons. A condition called Guillain-Barré Syndrome can also cause loss of myelin, but this is in the peripheral nerves and not in the CNS.

Using a Scan

The best way to actually see the damage caused by multiple sclerosis in the body is to use magnetic resonance imaging (MRI). This technique uses magnets to view the interior of the CNS.

What Is an MRI Scanner?

An MRI scanner is a big machine shaped like a tunnel that a person is put into. The scanning process relies on the fact that a powerful magnetic field, the area in which a magnetic force works, can cause water in the body to shift position. It does this by making charged particles in water, called hydrogen protons, line up in the direction of the field. Then radio waves are directed at the protons (positively charged particles) to knock them out of line. Finally, the radio waves are turned off, and the protons relax and line up again in the field. When they relax, the protons vibrate at a speed that the system can detect.

Reading the Human Body

The process the body undergoes within an MRI scanner has a big effect on it. The human body is made up of around 60 percent water, mostly trapped in cells. An MRI scanner "reads" the water in different human tissues and a computer program converts the data into images. These images show whether the tissues contain normal or abnormal cells, based on their water content.

MRIs can also be used in progressive forms of the disease to track CNS damage.

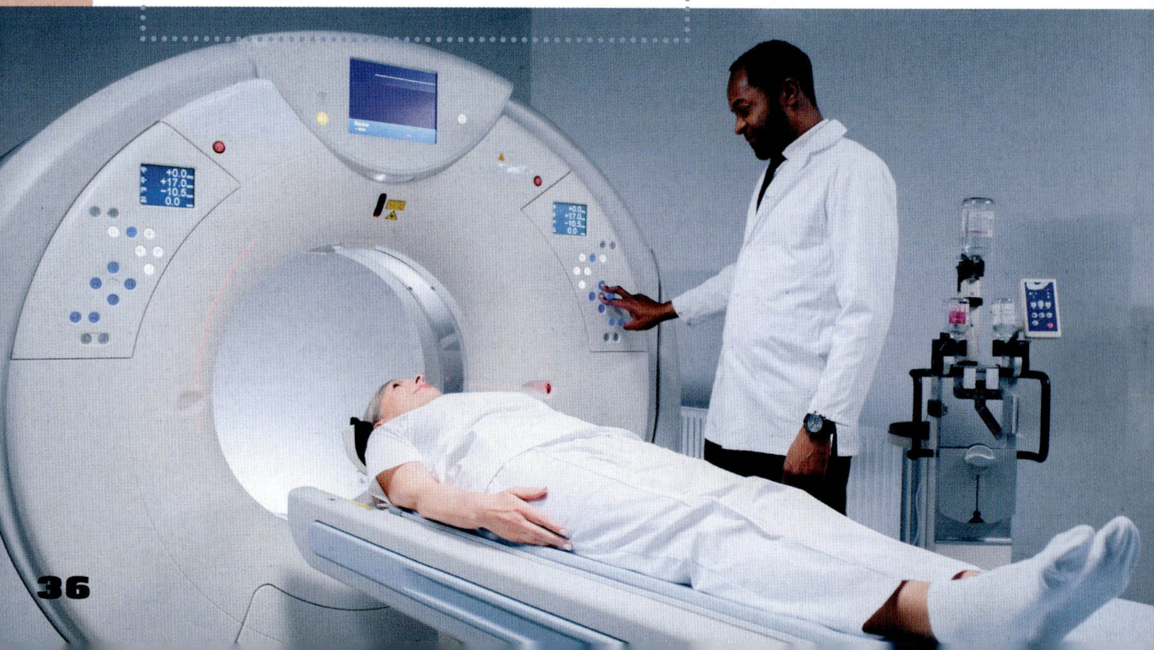

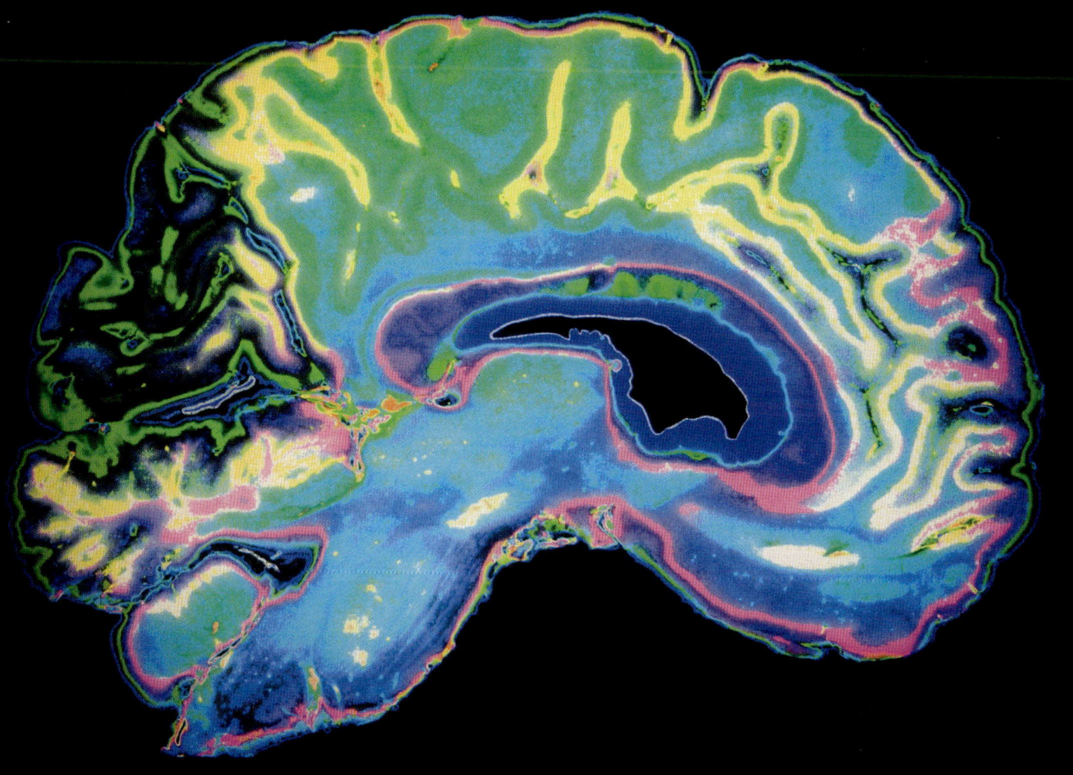

MRI scans can show highly detailed images of parts of the body, such as the brain, which helps doctors identify damage that may have been caused by multiple sclerosis.

Understanding Multiple Sclerosis

Myelin is a type of fat that repels water. Therefore, areas of tissue that have neurons with less myelin than usual, which is typical of multiple sclerosis plaques, hold onto more water than normal brain and spinal cord tissue. The MRI scanner takes many cross-sectional (slice) images in a session, and can piece them together into a three-dimensional (3-D) view of the affected area. The results of repeated scan visits can demonstrate the presence of myelin damage in different places and at different times. This can help confirm the diagnosis.

Further Testing

A series of MRI scans can show myelin damage in people, helping confirm multiple sclerosis. But in around 5 percent of people already diagnosed with the disease, MRI scans reveal no plaques. Additionally, plaques can be spotted in scans of people over the age of 50 that are a normal sign of aging rather than of multiple sclerosis. Other clinical tests are therefore used to assess changing myelin distribution in different ways without direct visualization.

Testing Spinal Fluid

A lumbar puncture, or spinal tap, is a procedure in which a neurologist inserts a needle into the space around the spinal cord, under local anesthetic. Neurologists use a syringe to carefully remove around one or two teaspoons (5–10 ml) of cerebrospinal fluid.

A Shock-Absorbing Fluid

Cerebrospinal fluid is a clear, colorless liquid that circulates around the brain and spinal cord. It normally acts as a shock absorber for the CNS against damage if the skull and vertebrae get knocked. It also circulates nutrients filtered from the blood that CNS cells need to remain healthy, and removes waste products from brain tissue. It may contain other substances as well, some of which can indicate multiple sclerosis.

While performing a lumbar puncture, surgeons must take care not to damage the spinal cord.

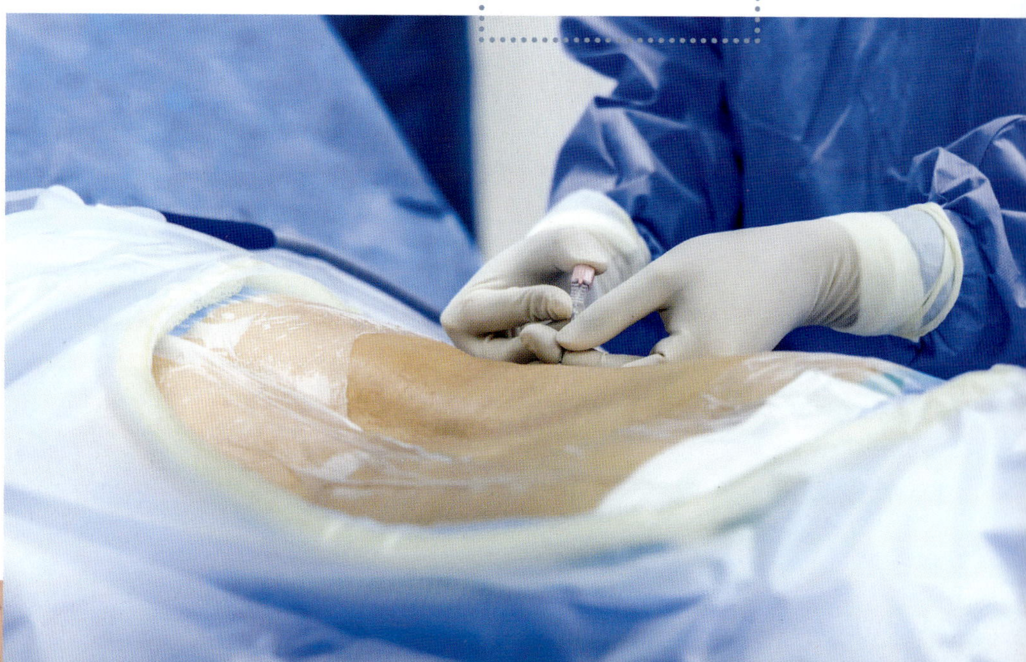

Understanding Multiple Sclerosis

To detect substances that can indicate multiple sclerosis, a sample of cerebrospinal fluid is sent to laboratories for examination by trained workers. In people with multiple sclerosis, the cerebrospinal fluid often shows raised levels of IgG antibodies produced by the body in response to T-cell attack. A test can reveal IgG antibodies of different sizes that indicate inflammation in the CNS. Lumbar puncture samples from people with multiple sclerosis also have raised levels of proteins produced when myelin is damaged by the immune system.

Further Tests

Another clinical test measures the time it takes for messages from a patient's eyes to reach their brain along the optic nerve. The neurologist places small pads called electrodes on the patient's head over the area of the brain where visual activity takes place. The patient sits in front of a screen that displays a changing checkerboard pattern of light and dark squares. If the optic nerve and CNS are not working normally due to axon myelin problems, the brain reacts more slowly than normal to the visual stimulus of the pattern change. Electrodes record this change as an evoked potential electrical signal. This is a measure of electrical activity in the brain in response to sight, touch, or sound.

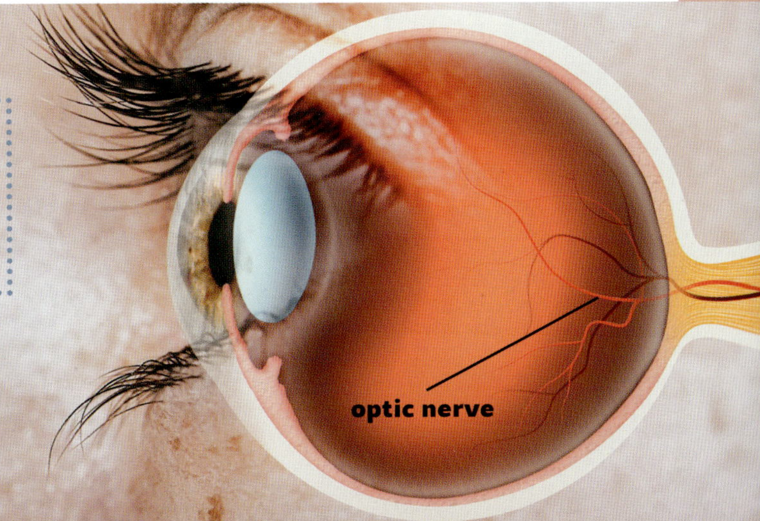

Testing the optic nerve of a patient is another way to find out if multiple sclerosis is present.

CHAPTER 4

Help with Multiple Sclerosis

Some diseases or conditions can be treated quite easily. For example, dracunculiasis is a painful disease caused by a parasitic worm. It has symptoms of intense burning pain, fever, and allergic reactions. It can be avoided by drinking clean water that is free of the worms. The incidence of this disease is very low. Other curable diseases, such as smallpox, have been totally wiped out. Multiple sclerosis cannot be cured like smallpox, but it can be managed using a variety of drug treatments. Doctors and neurologists decide on the best treatments to give, depending on what type of multiple sclerosis a patient has.

Reducing Relapses

Treatments called disease modifying therapies (DMTs) aim to prevent or reduce the number of relapses in relapsing-remitting multiple sclerosis. One class of DMT drugs is called beta-interferons. Your body makes proteins called interferons that reduce inflammation in tissues such as the CNS. Beta-interferons are humanmade versions that do the same thing. Different types are mostly injected under the skin, using a fine-needle syringe, once every few days or weeks. Beta-interferons can cause minor side effects such as headaches, muscle aches, or chills, but can reduce the number of relapses and the speed at which a person's disability progresses.

Botox is better known as a cosmetic treatment, but it can also be used to treat multiple sclerosis.

Killing T-Cells

Doctors may prescribe a DMT called alemtuzumab to people with active relapses of their multiple sclerosis. This drug kills T-cells to stop them from damaging the CNS. It can be highly effective for patients, reducing the number of relapses and the severity of the disease by around half. The problem is that alemtuzumab exposes people to infections, especially urinary tract and throat infections; can damage the thyroid gland, which is important in hormone production; and can also cause serious blood problems. Other types of DMTs include immunosuppressant drugs that hinder cell division, which is the way cells make copies of themselves to increase in number. Immunosuppressants can reduce the number of immune system cells and can be effective in some people with progressive multiple sclerosis.

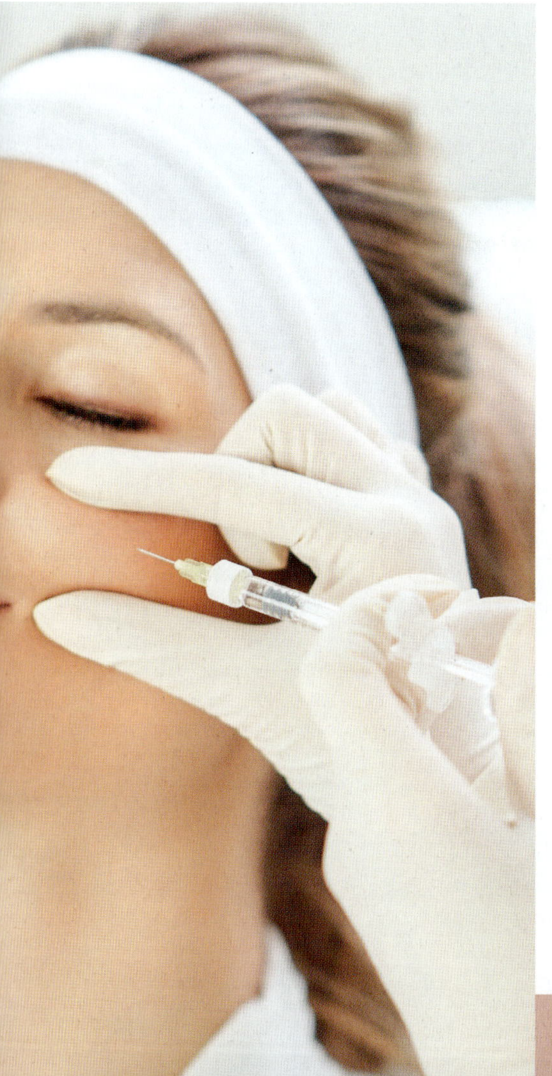

Understanding Multiple Sclerosis

Some drug treatments can help patients deal with their symptoms. For example, people may have urinary incontinence because their bladder muscles cannot hold onto urine or empty normally. One treatment is to inject Botox into the bladder wall. This drug is used in cosmetic surgery to reduce wrinkles on people's faces by blocking muscle contractions. Botox can help stop muscles from suddenly emptying the bladder, too. People with mobility problems may be prescribed dalfampridine, which is a drug that blocks tiny holes on exposed axons to help impulses move through. That enables patients to walk more easily.

Restoring Health

Many people with multiple sclerosis face difficulties in their daily lives, from loss of mobility and weakness to incontinence and difficulty swallowing. People with multiple sclerosis have many rehabilitation options to help them take control of their own lives and change them for the better. Rehabilitation means restoring someone's health through different therapies and training.

Physical Therapy

Healthcare workers called physical therapists work with patients to help improve the strength, control, and flexibility of their arms and legs through resistance exercises that force muscles to contract. The exercises increase the range of movement and prevents joint stiffness. Physical therapists also teach strategies to improve posture and leg position that increase stability when walking.

Physical therapists can massage, stretch, and move the legs of their patients by hand or by using gym equipment such as exercise balls.

Understanding Multiple Sclerosis

Many people with multiple sclerosis experience foot drop, which is the loss of tone in foot muscles, which makes it difficult to lift their feet properly. Wearing braces or splints helps keep the foot shape stable and reduces the chances of tripping or stumbling. Some people wear a leg band that produces mild electric shocks. This technique, called functional electrical stimulation (FES), produces nerve impulses that contract the foot muscles, reducing foot drop. Physical therapists can also help people choose mobility aids such as rolling walkers and scooters that help them move around when walking is challenging during relapses.

Speech Therapy

If people with multiple sclerosis have plaques in parts of the brain that control speech and swallowing, they may need the help of speech and swallowing therapists. These therapists evaluate patients for their individual needs, identifying specific places from lips to esophagus where changed movement is causing a problem. They may insert flexible, thin cameras called endoscopes to see problem areas inside the throat. Therapists then offer strategies to help, such as exercises that strengthen neck muscles. A stronger neck enables a patient to hold the head more upright to swallow better and avoid choking.

If multiple sclerosis affects a person's ability to walk, using a mobility aid can help them maintain their independence.

Healthy Eating

Eating healthily improves everyone's health, and this is no different for people with multiple sclerosis. There is no special diet for people with the disease. However, like everyone else, people with multiple sclerosis can change their energy level, digestive function, and overall health by eating well. Doctors recommend a diet high in fiber and low in fat, rich in vegetables and fruit, with less sugar and salt. A diet supplemented with omega-3 fatty acids from oily fish, cod-liver oil, and flaxseed oil, along with omega-6 fatty acids from sunflower oil, may improve myelin production.

Smoking and Multiple Sclerosis

Smoking tobacco has long been known to cause lung cancer and heart disease, but is now understood to worsen symptoms in people with multiple sclerosis. Every additional year of smoking after a multiple sclerosis diagnosis can speed up the shift to secondary-progressive multiple sclerosis by nearly 5 percent. Smokers with multiple sclerosis have a higher risk of relapse, more plaques on MRI, and greater disability. One possible reason is that smoking raises the risk of infections, thus stimulating more immune system activity.

Facing Facts

Vitamin D supplements benefit the CNS and immune system. However, individuals need to consult their doctors before taking them because they can worsen certain heart conditions and increase kidney stones in some people.

Resistance to movement from water can be used to increase strength and practice balance and coordination without falling.

People with multiple sclerosis may practice yoga and tai chi to increase mobility and calmness.

The Power of Exercise

When anyone does not exercise sufficiently, they face an increased risk of health issues ranging from weakness and shallow breathing to becoming overweight and having heart problems. People with multiple sclerosis who exercise often see physical improvements such as increased strength, better bladder and bowel control, and less fatigue. Exercise in water is especially helpful, partly because a person's buoyancy (ability to float) supports their weight so movement takes less effort.

Understanding Multiple Sclerosis

Some people with multiple sclerosis find that their symptoms improve after using complementary and alternative treatments. These are treatments whose effects are generally unproven by conventional scientific knowledge. One such treatment is acupuncture, where thin needles are pushed into the skin at particular locations. Another is magnetic field therapy, which uses strong magnetic pulses to stimulate charged particles in cells, and which some people claim reduces pain and inflammation.

Some people with multiple sclerosis find that alternative treatments such as acupuncture help to lessen symptoms.

Mental Health and Multiple Sclerosis

Dealing with the challenges of living with a chronic illness such as multiple sclerosis can take a toll on a person's mental health. Feelings of sadness, frustration, or grief related to a diagnosis, symptoms, and limitations as a result of the illness can make it very difficult to deal with day-to-day life.

LEADING TO ANXIETY

The uncertainty, unpredictability, and challenges of living with multiple sclerosis can cause feelings of anxiety and fear. Adjusting to the diagnosis, managing symptoms, and coping with the impact of the disease on daily life can be incredibly difficult. People may experience almost-constant worry and feelings of restlessness. Muscle tension, a rapid heartbeat, sweating, or trembling can be symptoms of anxiety.

People with multiple sclerosis can become very irritable and have difficulty relaxing.

LEADING TO DEPRESSION

Depression is common among people with multiple sclerosis. It is caused by having to deal with difficult physical symptoms and the changes that brings to all aspects of a person's life. Symptoms of depression may include continual sadness, a loss of interest or pleasure in activities, changes in appetite or weight, an inability to sleep or sleeping too much, fatigue, feelings of worthlessness or guilt, difficulty concentrating, and thoughts of self-harm or suicide.

More at Risk

People with multiple sclerosis are more at risk of suicide attempts than other people. Depression, pain, disability, and a sense of being cut off from the outside world can make people feel that life is not worth living. Feeling a burden on those around them can also bring about suicidal thoughts.

PHYSICAL LEADS TO PSYCHOLOGICAL

The physical symptoms of multiple sclerosis can have a huge psychological effect on people. Having to deal with pain and fatigue makes life seem a constant struggle. Added to that, problems with mobility, vision, digestive and bladder issues, and more, all make a person's quality of life much poorer. Those physical struggles often lead to mental health issues.

Adjusting to the diagnosis of multiple sclerosis and the difficulties associated with living with a chronic illness can be very challenging.

Dealing with Mental Health

Managing the psychological impact of multiple sclerosis often requires a variety of approaches, and different people will find that different tools work for them. Most obviously, help with the physical effects of the disease can reduce some of the emotional impact that the illness has on people. Developing strategies to tackle the anxiety and depression that often comes with multiple sclerosis can also help.

MANAGING STRESS

Stress can often feel overwhelming for people having to manage the unpredictable symptoms and uncertain future of multiple sclerosis. Strategies to manage anxiety have been shown to make dealing with a high-stress situation easier. They include practicing meditation, deep-breathing exercises, and muscle relaxation. Regular physical activity that matches a person's abilities has also been shown to improve mood, reduce anxiety and depression, and increase quality of life for people with multiple sclerosis. It is important that people always consult with their healthcare providers to create a safe exercise plan that is appropriate for them.

Setting time aside for things that make people feel good, such as a favorite hobby or spending time with family and friends, improves mental wellbeing.

EATING FOR EMOTIONAL HEALTH

Focusing on a healthy lifestyle is key to helping manage both the physical and psychological effects of multiple sclerosis (see pages 44–45). A healthy diet not only protects against some of the physical symptoms of the disease, it also helps maintain emotional wellbeing. Keeping hydrated is important for people with multiple sclerosis. Dehydration can make symptoms of fatigue and gut and bladder issues worse.

TALKING ABOUT DIFFICULTIES

Sometimes, people struggling with their mental health because of multiple sclerosis find counseling helpful. With a trained counselor, they can openly express emotions of frustration, grief, and anger that may be difficult to share with family and friends. Counseling can help them develop strategies for managing emotions, too.

Some people find group therapy helpful when tackling the emotional difficulties of multiple sclerosis. The therapy brings together people with the disease, so they can share their experiences and offer each other support.

Taking note of stresses in daily life, such as too much work and difficult time pressures, and trying to reduce them can help improve mental health. Setting realistic goals and learning to say "no" is also important for people with multiple sclerosis.

Asking for and having support from family and friends is very important for everyone, and particularly so for those dealing with a chronic disease.

CHAPTER 5

Living with Multiple Sclerosis

Living with any life-altering disease is a challenge. Part of the challenge with multiple sclerosis is the changing nature of the symptoms, along with the relapses and progressions which are part of the disease. Most people will experience increasing disability and difficulty carrying out daily tasks. Facing any challenge alone is not easy, so it really helps people with the disease to have a support network.

A Team of People

A support network includes family doctors, neurologists, physical therapists, and other healthcare professionals. These professionals can alter therapies depending on the changing needs of the patient over time. But they cannot be present all the time, so another key part of a support network is the caregiver.

Healthcare professionals may provide additional support at home to people more severely affected by mobility issues.

Facing Facts

Adding a walk-in shower rather than a regular shower cubicle to a home can make washing easier. For people who struggle to hold regular utensils, specially designed utensils with easy-to-grip, larger handles and angled tips may allow them to feed themselves more easily.

The Role of Therapists

Occupational therapists are another important element of the support network. Their job is to make it easier for people with multiple sclerosis to go about their daily activities, ranging from washing and dressing to cooking and taking part in leisure activities. For example, installing ramps and widening doors in a home can make it easier for someone with multiple sclerosis to move their mobility scooter around. Grab rails and seats can make it safer for them to lower themselves onto the toilet or take a shower by themselves.

Understanding Multiple Sclerosis

Support groups are also part of the support network for people with multiple sclerosis. There are many networks of fellow sufferers who meet up online or in person at halls, hospitals, or colleges. These groups can be a great help for people. The groups give people the chance to share tips on dealing with symptoms of the disease and to talk about the challenges, successes, and frustrations of life with multiple sclerosis.

A Plan for Dealing with Multiple Sclerosis

There are many daily hurdles that people with multiple sclerosis have to overcome. People can manage by using strategies to help themselves, and also by reaching out to other people. Sharing experiences, emotions, and practical tips for moderating symptoms of multiple sclerosis with other people who suffer from the disease can be an enormous help.

Strategies That Help

Avoiding isolation by going out and being part of society helps people live a fuller, happier life. However, leaving the home can present challenges. People with multiple sclerosis find that strategies that have helped others living with the disease can help them too.

Dealing with mobility: It can be tricky and slow to walk unaided or using canes, crutches, or mobility scooters. That means many journeys need to be planned in advance and extra time allowed to reach destinations.

Dealing with toilet issues: Incontinence, or the experience of wetting or soiling yourself, can be a real issue for people with multiple sclerosis. There are various strategies to help reduce stress related to incontinence:

- Planning frequent stops and knowing the location of easily accessible toilets when out of the house
- Wearing an incontinence pad that can absorb the urine or stool (solid waste) without soaking clothes
- Wearing pants that can easily be taken off, such as pants with an elastic waistband
- Carrying a spare set of underwear, pads, catheters, and other incontinence-related needs at all times

Facing Facts

Some people with incontinence resulting from multiple sclerosis use catheters, or tubes into their urethras (urinary tracts), so they can empty their urine into a toilet or into bags they may wear under their clothing. Using catheters can help people control the emptying of their bladder, but they can also increase the chances of getting urinary infections. These infections cause painful inflammation and may require antibiotics.

Dealing with heat: Heat worsens the symptoms for many people with multiple sclerosis without actually causing more loss of myelin or nerve damage. There are ways to manage particularly hot days. These include:

- Wearing lightweight, loose-fitting clothing made of natural fibers such as cotton
- Being active at cooler times of the day
- Installing air conditioning or fans to cool room interiors on hot days
- Taking long, cooling baths to lower the body temperature when overheating becomes a problem.

Wheelchair users find that they must allow extra time and organization when planning a day out.

People often find incontinence embarrassing. But they shouldn't—after all, incontinence is at least an occasional problem for around one in seven women in the United States.

Employment and Multiple Sclerosis

For people with multiple sclerosis, going to work can be challenging. It can be difficult to predict when symptoms may worsen, and inevitably that makes holding down a job difficult. People with the disease must also manage difficult physical and emotional health problems while at work, and finding a job that accommodates those issues may not be easy.

DIFFICULT JOBS MADE HARDER

We have learned that multiple sclerosis causes problems with the brain that lead to issues with memory, focus, and information processing. Those issues can have an impact on different parts of a job, from understanding instructions and remembering information to problem solving, decision making, and managing more than one task at once. That makes working in demanding or complex work environments difficult, and often impossible.

ENERGY FOR WORK

Fatigue is one of the most common symptoms of multiple sclerosis and can make a normal working day debilitating. It can be hard for people with multiple sclerosis to find the necessary energy and levels of concentration to carry out their work. The disease can affect productivity at work, and people may struggle to keep their focus, remain alert, and perform tasks effectively due to fatigue.

PHYSICAL TASKS

Some jobs that require certain physical strength and mobility are difficult for people with multiple sclerosis to do. The symptoms of weakness, spasticity, balance problems, tremors (or shaking), and mobility difficulties that go with the disease often make it impossible to do many manual jobs. Tasks that need good coordination and dexterity (the ability to carry out complicated movements with the fingers) may also be difficult for people with multiple sclerosis.

Standing for long periods of time can be an issue, which makes some service-based jobs, such as working in retail or in a café, a problem.

Adding to the Stress

Coping with the challenges of dealing with multiple sclerosis in the workplace can add to a person's already-high levels of stress, anxiety, and depression. That additional stress and pressure can worsen both their mental and physical symptoms. Often, people with multiple sclerosis find that they need to change their line of work to deal with the impact the disease has on them, and some people find they need to give up work altogether because they cannot find a role that accommodates their illness.

Still today, a number of workplaces have not been properly adapted to accommodate people with disabilities.

Dealing with Employment

While multiple sclerosis can make the world of work challenging, it is possible to have a successful career while dealing with the disease. People who have managed to do so say that finding an accommodating workplace, supportive employers, and help from healthcare providers has made going to work manageable.

TALKING ABOUT MULTIPLE SCLEROSIS AT WORK

Communicating openly and honestly with employers about multiple sclerosis and support needed in the workplace is vital. It helps the person with the disease manage at work. It also helps the employer better understand the condition, and make changes where needed. People may need adjustments made to their working environment, such as making a workspace easy to navigate with a wheelchair. They may also need a flexible schedule, which can allow for times when symptoms are worse. People may also need help with certain tasks that the disease makes difficult.

CHANGING THE JOB

Sometimes, it may be necessary to redesign a job after a person has been diagnosed with multiple sclerosis, or give some more-difficult parts of their role to another employee. By making roles more flexible, such as introducing part-time roles or job sharing, continuing to work can be made easier for people with the disease. A part-time role is often more realistic for people who are struggling with fatigue and may need to manage medical appointments and treatments alongside their job.

Ensuring that the workplace environment is accessible makes going to work far easier for people with disabilities.

For working people with multiple sclerosis, putting in place a good self-care program to manage symptoms is vital. That includes taking breaks when needed and setting realistic goals that are not too demanding. It includes making time for rest and relaxation, and also maintaining health as best as possible through a healthy diet and appropriate exercise.

Today, more and more companies are offering flexible working arrangements, which helps people with multiple sclerosis have a career.

Respect and Support

Being able to continue working can be one of the key strategies that helps people with multiple sclerosis manage their mental health. With good communication between employers, employees, and healthcare providers, it is possible to create workplaces that make beginning and maintaining a satisfying career possible for people with the disease.

CONCLUSION

Multiple Sclerosis and the Future

There is great hope for future treatment of multiple sclerosis. Gene therapy is very experimental and stem cell therapy is in its infancy. Yet both are exciting possibilities for treating the disease and lessening its symptoms. One day soon, perhaps these will be used with well-established drug and rehabilitation therapies.

Ongoing Research

Scientists, neurologists, and epidemiologists working for charities, universities, and hospitals are searching for, testing, and ensuring the safety of new treatments. Many of the charities are part of the Progressive MS Alliance. This is a global network of charities united in speeding up diagnosis, monitoring, and developing treatments for progressive multiple sclerosis, which has been trickier to diagnose quickly and to treat than the relapsing form.

Finding New Treatments

Here are a few recent ideas that might be put to use in the future:

Neuroprotection: The aim of neuroprotection is to keep neurons alive and active, even if their myelin is damaged. One class of drugs, called sodium channel blockers, prevents the buildup of sodium in the brain that is linked to nerve damage. One trial using a sodium channel blocker called phenytoin, which is often used to treat epilepsy, showed that its use reduced damage to the optic nerve by 30 percent during optic neuritis.

Immunomodulators: Several new disease-modifying treatments called immunomodulators are showing promise in targeting the specific immune system cells that appear to control the shift from relapsing to progressive multiple sclerosis. For example, in one trial, a drug called siponimod reduced disability progression by 21 percent in volunteers with secondary-progressive multiple sclerosis. It also reduced shrinking of brain tissue caused by plaques.

There are hopes that science will find more effective treatments for multiple sclerosis, and ultimately a cure.

Understanding Multiple Sclerosis

Investigators from The International Multiple Sclerosis Microbiome Study have been collecting stool samples from people with multiple sclerosis. Their aim is to identify the types and numbers of bacteria the stools contain. The stomach and intestines contain millions of bacteria that are thought to be extremely important in establishing and maintaining immune balance in people. The feeling is that certain species of bacteria may protect people from multiple sclerosis, but others may cause immune attack on the CNS and put people at risk of developing the disease. Scientists working on this project have found multiple species of bacteria that are linked with multiple sclerosis.

"Life with multiple sclerosis is difficult. That's why there is always new research with the hope of improving the lives of people dealing with the disease."

Glossary

accessible able to be easily approached, entered, or used by people with disabilities

accommodating willing to make adjustments in order to meet the needs of others

adaptive keyboards keyboards with features that accommodate people with physical disabilities, such as larger keys

antibiotics medications used to treat bacterial infections by killing bacteria or preventing their growth

antihistamine a type of medication that relieves allergic symptoms such as itching and sneezing

anxiety a state of fear or worry

bacteria tiny organisms that can cause infections or diseases

bladder an organ in the pelvis that stores urine

bone marrow the soft, spongy tissue found within bones

chromosomes threadlike structures found in cells that carry genetic information

chronic illness a long-lasting or persistent health condition or disease

cognitive relating to thought, memory, or understanding

complementary describes treatment used alongside conventional medical treatments

coordination the ability to synchronize movements, mainly of the legs and arms

cystic fibrosis a hereditary genetic disease that affects the lungs and digestive system

debilitating causing severe problems that make normal physical or emotional functioning difficult

deficiency a lack of something essential for health, such as vitamins

depression feelings of sadness and hopelessness

designated set aside for a specific purpose

diagnosed identified as having a particular condition, illness, or disease

digestive function the process of breaking down food, absorbing nutrients, and removing waste from the body

disability a physical or mental impairment that limits normal activities

epilepsy a neurological disorder that causes seizures due to abnormal electrical brain activity

extracurricular activities undertaken outside of regular academic or work responsibilities, such as sports, clubs, hobbies, and volunteer work

fertilizes combines sperm and egg cells to create an embryo

filtered passed through a barrier to remove impurities

formal following established rules

genes tiny parts of every living thing that carry instructions for its development and function

grief intense sorrow, sadness, or emotional pain experienced in response to loss

harvested collected or gathered

hereditary passed down from one generation to another

hormone a chemical messenger produced in the body

immune response the body's defensive reaction to potentially harmful invaders

immunosuppressant drugs medications that suppress the immune system's activity

impacting influencing or affecting something in a significant way

inclusive encouraging the inclusion of diverse groups of people

incontinence the inability to control bladder or bowel movements

inflammation redness, swelling, heat, and pain in the body in response to injury, infection, or irritation

informal relaxed and unofficial

intestines the long, tubelike organs of the digestive system

intolerance a negative reaction or sensitivity to certain substances, foods, or environmental factors

isolation room a room used to isolate people who are at risk of infection or at risk of infecting others

kidney stones hard deposits that sometimes form in the kidneys

limitations restrictions on abilities, functions, or activities

migrate to move from one place to another

misconceptions false or mistaken ideas about something

mobility the ability to move or travel freely and independently

modifications changes or adjustments made to something to make it more suitable

muscle contraction the process of tightening or shortening muscle fibers to produce movement

mutation a permanent change in the DNA sequence of a gene

neurological relating to the nervous system, including the brain, spinal cord, nerves, and sensory organs

nutrients substances needed for growth, development, and good health

parasite an organism that lives on or inside another organism, often causing harm or disease

predict to estimate the likelihood of something happening

psychological relating to mental processes, emotions, behaviors, or experiences

reflexes automatic responses or movements of the body in response to stimuli

remission a period of time during which symptoms of a disease or condition are reduced or not present

respiration the process of breathing, involving the intake of oxygen and the release of carbon dioxide by the lungs

seizures sudden, abnormal electrical activity in the brain that can cause stiffness, twitching, or limpness in the body

social interactions verbal and nonverbal behavior between people

speech-to-text software computer software that converts spoken words into written text

stereotypes oversimplified judgments about people based on their characteristics

stigma negative attitudes, beliefs, or perceptions toward people based on their characteristics

stimulus something that triggers a response or reaction in a person

suicide the act of intentionally taking one's own life, often as a result of severe emotional distress

supplements dietary products containing vitamins, minerals, herbs, or other substances

transplanted surgically transferred from one location to another

urinary tracts the organs and structures involved with the production of urine and its removal from the body

viruses tiny infectious organisms that can replicate, or copy themselves, inside other organisms and cause disease

Find Out More

Books

DeSilva, Katherine A. *Dancing Together—Dads Get MS Too: A Life with Multiple Sclerosis*. Pumpkin Vines, 2023.

Gleason, Trevis L. *Living Well with Multiple Sclerosis*. Coffee Town Press, 2024.

Menara, Wendy J. *Silence of Shame: A Child Caring for Her Bedridden Mother*. Turtle Mountain Stories, 2020.

Websites

For facts and statistics on multiple sclerosis, visit:
www.healthline.com/health/multiple-sclerosis

What is multiple sclerosis? Find out at:
https://kidshealth.org/en/kids/multiple-sclerosis.html

The Multiple Sclerosis Association of America has a lot of information about the condition. Log on at:
https://mymsaa.org

Publisher's note to educators and parents:
All the websites featured above have been carefully reviewed to ensure that they are suitable for students. However, many websites change often, and we cannot guarantee that a site's future contents will continue to meet our high standards of educational value. Please be advised that students should be closely monitored whenever they access the Internet.

Index

alternative treatments 28, 45
antibodies 16–17, 39
anxiety 46, 48, 55, 60
axons 8–9, 41

bacteria 8, 16–17, 59–60
beta-interferons 40
biotin 28
bladder 4, 6, 41, 45, 47, 49, 52, 60–61
Botox 40–41
brain 4–5, 8–9, 11–13, 23, 25, 28, 31, 37–39, 43, 54, 58–60

causes 8, 16–18, 20, 28, 35, 54, 60
cerebrospinal fluid 38–39
chemotherapy 26–27
chromosomes 20, 22, 60
cognitive changes 6
constipation 6
coordination 30, 34, 44, 54, 60

depression 6, 47–48, 55, 60
diet 44, 48–49, 57
disease-modifying therapies 40
dizziness 6

education 12, 14–15, 33
employment 54, 56
environmental factors 18–19, 21, 61
epidemiologists 10, 18, 58
exercise 15, 42–43, 45, 48, 57

family 18, 20, 31–33, 48–50
functional electrical stimulation 43

gene therapy 22–23, 58
genes 5, 20–23, 61
grief 46, 49, 61

health 17–18, 20, 30, 33, 42, 44–49, 54, 57, 60
heat, problems with 4, 53, 61

immune system 8–10, 21, 23–27, 35, 39, 41, 44, 59, 61
incontinence 6, 34, 41–42, 52–53, 61
infections 5, 16, 27, 35, 41, 44, 52, 60
inflammation 11, 20, 26, 39–40, 45, 61

lumbar puncture 38–39

medication 28, 60–61
memory 5, 12, 54, 60
mobility 9, 13, 30, 32, 41–43, 45, 47, 51–52, 54, 61
mononucleosis 17
mood 6, 48
MRIs 36–37
mutations 20–22
myelin 8–9, 11, 20, 23, 28–29, 35, 37–39, 44, 53, 58

neurologists 25, 38, 40, 50, 58
neurons 5, 8–9, 23, 28, 35, 37, 58
NR1H3 gene 20
numbness 6

pain 4–6, 30, 32, 34, 40, 45, 47, 61
plaques 8–9, 37–38, 43–44, 59
primary-progressive 7
progression 50, 59
proteins 16, 20, 39–40

rehabilitation 42, 58
relapses 7, 17, 40–41, 43, 50
relapsing-remitting 7, 9

signals 5, 28
smoking 44
social connections 30–32
spasticity 6, 13, 54
speech, problems with 4–6, 8, 15, 31, 34, 43
spinal cord 5, 8, 25, 37–38
spinal tap 38
stem cell therapy 25, 28, 58
stress 15, 48–49, 52, 55
sunlight 10, 18
support 14, 18, 30, 32–33, 45, 49–51, 56–57
symptoms 4–9, 15, 17, 19, 23, 30, 32–35, 40–41, 44–58, 60

T-cells 8, 23, 26, 28, 41
treatments 28, 40–41, 45, 56, 58–60
triggers 23

viruses 8, 16–17, 22–23, 27
vision, problems with 4, 34, 47
vitamin D 18, 23, 29, 44

walking, problems with 6, 8–9, 42–43
weakness 6, 13, 19, 30, 34–35, 42, 45, 54

About the Author

Sarah Eason has written many books for children and young adults. Researching and writing this book has highlighted the complexities of multiple sclerosis, from its causes to its treatments, and the challenges that people with the disease face. She hopes this book is an informative, helpful, and compassionate resource for readers interested in the topic or affected by it.